MORGAN DERBYSHIRE MIDDLESEX GLOUCESTERSHIRE

ESSEX

ESSEX YORKSHIRE NORTHAMPTONSHIRE LANCASHIRE

This book is dedicated to A.G. (Bert) Robinson,
formerly of Northamptonshire and for many years
Cricket Professional at Radley, a man of
infinite wisdom and a splendid cricketer in all
senses of the word.

This book could not have been written without
constant reference to WISDEN, The Cricketer's
Almanack now published by Gollancz. Thanks are
also due to John Cooper who checked the
manuscript and whose encyclopaedic knowledge
of cricket facts was invaluable.

Published in 1985 by
BELL & HYMAN LIMITED
Denmark House
37–39 Queen Elizabeth Street
London SE1 2QB

British Library Cataloguing in Publication Data

Cooper, Leo
    Leo and Jilly Cooper on cricket.
    1. Cricket—Anecdotes, facetiae, satire, etc.
    I. Title   II. Cooper, Jilly
    796.35′8′0207   GV919

ISBN: 0 7135 2537 1

Designed by Peter Hardman
Typeset by August Filmsetting, St Helens
Produced in Great Britain by Purnell & Sons Ltd, Paulton.

LEO & JILLY COOPER ON
CRICKET

PICTURES BY ross

LEO & JILLY COOPER ON

CRICKET

PICTURES BY ross

BELL & HYMAN

Contents

Origins of the Game

It is not entirely clear how the game of cricket started. Whoever invented it, some time before 1300, seems to have chosen to remain anonymous. Perhaps he never really thought it would catch on. Perhaps when he tried explaining it to his medieval friends (you stand in front of two sticks, brandishing a piece of willow, and I throw a piece of leather at you, and then you run up and down), they failed to foresee its potential for worldwide appeal, national media coverage and opportunity to bring him fame and fortune.

Nonetheless, it did catch on. It is mentioned in Edward I's wardrobe accounts in 1300. Not, unfortunately, that the wardrobe accounts tell us what it would have cost the king to buy a pair of pads at the time. But at least it tells us that distinctive clothing was already part of the act. By 1683 the length of the pitch had been established at 22 yards, and the form of the wicket as two stumps and a bail. All over the land, or certainly from Guildford to Maidstone, people had got down to the serious aspects of enjoying cricket, such as formulating rules and getting fined for playing on Sundays.

By the eighteenth century the game was widespread, and a full score survives from a match in 1744 at the Artillery Ground featuring Kent against All England. Unless All England was a euphemism for Guildford, this suggests that cricket had started to find favour nationwide. 1744 was also the year when the laws of cricket were formally written down, although everybody must already have had a rough idea of what they were. For instance, most cricket players could probably go through the motions of the toss, before looking up the rules to read: 'Ye pitching of ye first wicket is to be determined by ye cast of a piece of money.'

There was also the tricky question even then of just how much power the umpire had. The rules stated 'each umpire is the sole judge of all nips, catches, ins and outs, good or bad runs', which just goes to show that eighteenth century umpires (like so many we could name) tended to think they were absolutely omnipotent. In fact apart from a few details, such as the addition of a third stump, the shape of the bat and the scoring methods, remarkably little has changed.

The romantics among us however like to think that cricket really began in 1750 at Hambledon on Broad Halfpenny Down. At that time the general verdict on the sport was:

'Cricket is certainly a very good and wholesome exercise,
yet it may be abused if either great or little people
make it their business.'

Medium sized people, who treat it as a wholesome exercise, not as a business, can and do of course continue to find it very good.

The MCC

The MCC appears at this
early stage of the book
because it seemed a good
idea to get it out of the way.

The Marylebone Cricket Club is the most famous cricket club in the
world as well as being cricket's most respected body. From its headquarters
at Lords its influence stretches worldwide. Until recently all first class
touring sides from the United Kingdom played abroad under MCC colours.

There are several ways of becoming a member of the MCC. The best way
is to persuade your father to put you down for membership at birth. If you
apply later in life you usually have to wait several years to be elected. You
can become a member by playing a series of qualifying matches, but this is
a difficult and risky method – particularly if you are no good. It is also
possible to be elected an honorary member. However, this is an exceptional
privilege and involves first having an immensely distinguished cricketing
career.

In recent years the influence and standing of the MCC has waned rather.
This is partly because the game has become much more commercialised. In
an attempt to run with the hounds the MCC has increased its membership
limits and let in a lot of people who spend most of their time either
wandering among the seats in the middle of overs or assaulting the
umpires, or propping up the bar drinking gin and discussing 'horse back
riding'.

Influential school sides like to arrange an annual fixture against the
MCC. For these matches the MCC supplies sides composed of non-benders
and surly young groundstaff from Lords who have been rounded up at the
last minute. This doesn't matter, though. From a school's or club's point of
view the most important thing is to have the glory of the MCC appearing
on their fixture list, rather than necessarily to have any particularly
glorious players appearing on their ground.

Although the MCC has always welcomed people who aren't very good at
cricket it does still have grave reservations about admitting people who
are women – even if their qualities at square leg, not to mention their vital
statistics, are beyond criticism. An England women's side did recently play
at Lords, after a long unseemly row, but the Pavilion is still a strictly male
preserve. Lords and Ladies is *not* an idea that goes down well with the
MCC. And anyway no woman would be seen dead in their colours.

The County Championship

The seventeen first class counties who compete in the County Championship form the hard core of professional cricket. The championship itself is a competition with just the sort of baffling and complicated scoring system one might expect from a game like cricket. A county can gain 16 points for a win (well, 16 is a good roundish number), and then there are all sorts of other complicated points awarded for various bonuses and things like run rates etc. Looking at the scoreboard will never give you any idea about who is actually winning. The best way to find this out is to ask a handy neighbourhood maths graduate with a pocket calculator on him, or read the next day's papers.

The counties themselves have varying claims to fame. Yorkshire is famous for having been very successful in the past and, more recently, for being involved in hysterical squawking matches about Boycott. Glamorgan is famous for having produced the only Welsh clarinet player to captain England (Tony Lewis); and for always having lots of players called Jones. Essex, although generally rather a good side, is remembered for having allowed Holmes and Sutcliffe to make 555 runs against them in a first wicket stand for Yorkshire. That was in 1932. The fact that they have since carried away many of cricket's highest honours has not erased the memory. Cricket is like that.

Kent is best known for wicket keepers. There are the good ones, such as L.E.G. Ames, Godfrey Evans and Alan Knott. And then there was Catt, who once let a record 48 byes through in one innings. He has not been forgotten either. Gloucestershire's most unforgettable player was of course Dr W.G. Grace, who lives on in rather more glorious memory as the patron saint of cricket.

Middlesex has the best known cricket ground, at Lords. Surrey has to make do with the second best known at the Oval. In spite of its interesting ambience of gasworks, grammar schools and noisy gentlemen from Brixton, the Oval never seems to generate quite the same romance as Lords. Somehow Surrey just isn't very memorable. Angry Surrey supporters may protest, saying remember the Bedsers, Brockwell (remember Brockwell?), J.H. Edrich (yes), Hayes E.G. and Hayward T. (yes), Hobbs (of course), Hitch (perhaps), J.C. Laker (of course, except he was a Yorkshireman), A.J. Macintyre (who could ever believe this man was a Cricketer of The Year 1958?), P.B.H. May, M.J. Stewart, and last but not least Tony Lock. Well, we do remember them. But not particularly Surrey.

Hampshire has a good record of ex-public school skippers. Not so good of championship wins (only once). The two things are probably not connected and anyway Hampshire is the birthplace of cricket and a likeable side. Somerset is also a likeable, and an increasingly successful side, but with a more eccentric breed of supporter. Many of them of course are perfectly normal people. It isn't that you *have* to be a white-hatted, cider drinking farmer with an extremely loud voice to support Somerset. It's just that a lot of people who do, are. Somerset, incidentally, like Northants and Sussex, have never won the championship.

Sussex has a lovely ground at Hove, fresh with sea air and pensioners. The ground has a close, family atmosphere and a slightly Victorian feeling, a bit like some of the cricket they play.

Nottinghamshire have a Test match ground in Trent Bridge. They also produced the famous Gunn family, of Gunn and Moore cricket bat fame. Worcestershire were once known as Fostershire because so many chaps from the family Foster (seven in fact) played for them. Also they always used to play host to touring sides in their first match (but were never known as Hostershire). Leicestershire are very efficient and businesslike. Northants recently had an Hon. playing for them. Warwickshire (who have a Test match ground at Edgebaston) and Derbyshire are workmanlike, midland, middle of order clubs.

Being Yorkshire supporters, we have tried not to mention Lancashire. But, grudgingly, we have to admit that Lancashire was until recently quite a passable side. They were, among other things, the last county to insist that their captain should be an amateur. He was required to stay in a different hotel from his players and to emerge from a different pavilion gate when going out to bat. In fact it is quite surprising that his players got to know who he was at all.

To represent one's county is a grand achievement, whichever county it is. It will also be an achievement that lives on. The great heroes of county cricket have the heartwarming knowledge that they will be written about in Wisdens, and exaggerated about in pubs and bars for years to come. The reward for being good at cricket is glorious immortality.

Minor Counties, etc.

Minor Counties

The minor counties and the second XIs from the first class counties play in two divisions – Eastern and Western. Spectators at these matches usually consist of the players' families and a few locals who seem to have strayed in by mistake after a run of bad luck at the bingo hall. This is not because the cricket played at this level is uninteresting. Often it is first rate, even though it isn't first class.

The players tend to be a combination of the recently-were-very-good and hope-they-soon-will-be-very-good. The first category still play a civilised game, chalking up elegant hundreds and happy memories. The second category play a tensely competitive game, trying hard to prove that elegant hundreds and happy memories will soon be theirs.

Leagues

Although there are leagues of various sorts all over the country, when we talk of League cricket we generally mean the dour game played among the former mill towns of Lancashire and Yorkshire. This is played mainly by amateurs, even though there is quite a lot of money at stake and the players do get paid for scoring fifties or hundreds or for taking five wickets. In this area of the game scoring 49 runs and taking four wickets in a match tends to be seen as a maddeningly disappointing performance.

Public School Cricket

Cricket was adopted very early by the gentry. The public schools, with their superlative wickets and often ex-professional coaches, were a seed bed for some of the greatest cricketers. However in the old days there was a rigid distinction between amateurs and professionals – Gentlemen and Players. As a result public school Gentlemen could not be paid for playing

even in county or international cricket. By about twenty years ago things had reached a ridiculous state, where only a few very rich people could afford both to be Gentlemen and play serious cricket. Now thank goodness the distinction between amateurs and professionals has gone. All the players muck in together, stay in the same hotels, share rooms together and are treated as equals. In 1984 no fewer than eleven public school educated players represented England. They may have lost their Gentlemanly status, but it is to be welcomed that they have rejoined the Players.

Amateur and Village Cricket

There are thousands of cricket clubs all over the British Isles. Towns, villages, banks, the Services, Old Boys and pubs all have their sides and their fixture lists. Not all of them however have grounds to play on. This might at first sight seem to be a major disadvantage. However, in fact, the wandering sides who travel about looking for teams *with* grounds to play against are the cream of the amateur game.

There are of course obvious advantages to never being local to the place where you play. That way, for example, it will never be *your* local councillor who turns nasty after your best six has destroyed his greenhouse. And it won't be *your* groundsman who goes into a nervous decline after your heroic attempt at a catch somehow lifted a foot of turf from his perfect square. As a visiting player you need have no inhibitions. (You just may not be asked back.)

Whatever the reasons, the wandering sides are some of the best, and they choose names that show off their homeless status such as I Zingari (meaning the gypsies), The Nomads, The Buccaneers, The Eton Ramblers, The Radley Rangers and the Uppingham Rovers. Another aspect of wandering teams betrayed by these names is that they tend to be upper middle class and dominated by the public schools. However you do also have to be good at cricket to play for the club. Not even a bona fide earl with a whole wardrobe full of club ties will last long unless his batting is at least as impressive as his ancestry. If he gets into the Free Foresters he will not only have to bat or bowl well, he will also have to wear the Club Blazer at luncheon and its colours on the field. It's no cheap life being part of a smart wandering team.

Village cricket of course is a legend unto itself. On any Saturday or Sunday afternoon in the summer you can drive through almost any village in England and find a cricket match in progress. Cricket started among ordinary people in country hamlets, and it still flourishes there. Many of the prettiest cricket grounds are to be found in the small towns and villages, and the great majority feature some or all of the essential clichés: a not too well cut outfield, a little clubhouse, a church tower thrusting through the woods in the background, an open-armed pub just over the road, a ring of chestnut trees round the ground and, in the corner by the tumbledown shed where the mower is kept, an old and rusting horse-drawn roller.

Around the ground, under the shade of the trees, there are benches

in various stages of dilapidation supporting gnarled spectators in a similar condition. Sometimes there will be a crescent of parked cars twinkling in the sunlight – many of them belonging to passers-by who, with their collapsible steel-framed chairs arranged around the exhaust pipe of their most treasured possession, will be settling in to gargantuan picnics. And where better, after all, for the Thermos set to enjoy their leisure than against a background of shifting white-clad cricketers, with only the occasional ripple of applause or gasp of amazement to distract their attention, and only the tiniest, almost piquant, risk that a cricket ball might suddenly land in their coronation chicken?

Out on the pitch, however, matters are far more tense, and the games are often fiercely contested. Special fixtures between certain villages can take on the character of veritable blood matches. The age of the players can be anything from seventeen to seventy seven, but their enthusiasm is uniformly high, and a joy to watch.

Not much has changed over the decades in village cricket. It is true to say that the typical one-padded and grey-trousered slogger of yesteryear has now given way in places to a more carefully attired breed of amateur cricketer. This is not however an indication of any particular increase in the skill of the players. It is more a tribute to the marketing skills of sports equipment manufacturers.

Very often the match will continue 'until the shadows lengthen and the evening comes'. Or at any rate until pub opening hour comes – whichever is the sooner. It is then that the rivalries, disappointments, triumphs and near-misses of the day can be given their essential slow-motion action replays over brimming pints and packets of cheese and onion crisps.

Cricket is an essential part of village life – its true meaning only ever fully understood by those who have sat out hours and days and weeks of their lives in a boundary deckchair, or welded to an old bench at the edge of a sun-dappled ground in the shires.

Test Matches

These are of course the ultimate in cricket. Passions run high about Test matches – even in England. Spectators at close finishes have been known to die of heart attacks, to eat their umbrella handles, to riot, to attack the players and even to dig up the pitch at night.

All sorts of surprising people ranging from pale young fellows in the computer programming department to elderly dentist's receptionists and criminal looking teenagers in the bus queue, show a sudden, uncharacteristic interest in whether it is raining at Headingley. Or they keep making surreptitious phone calls to find out whether Gavaskar has reached his hundred.

Besides England, the other Test status countries are Australia, India, Pakistan, the West Indies, Sri Lanka and New Zealand. Until very recently these last two were barely regarded as being of Test match status. Since then they have convincingly embarrassed the English side. Enough said.

South Africa used to be included in Test series before political issues sadly intervened and deprived us of the chance to watch some of their magnificent cricketers. It was in South Africa in 1939 that an experiment was made to play a 'timeless' cricket match. It went on for ten days and even then ended in a draw, because of rain. Since then, it has been firmly decided that five days, or even often one day, is quite timeless enough.

The real magic of a Test match is to sit among the crowds at Lords on a summer evening, the packed stands tense and hushed. Even the drunkards in the tavern are silent as Hall or Griffiths makes a thirty yard run up to bowl to another white-flannelled hero. There is the sweet crack of ball on bat, and a sudden burst of activity in the field, sending the pigeons flapping into the air, as the red ball streaks across the turf to thwack against the white palings in front of the Pavilion. A roar of applause. The figures on the scoreboard flicker. Four more runs. Time to settle into your seat and wait for the bowler to plod back to his mark, the ground humming with interest and then falling silent again. This is great drama. This is cricket at its best.

And sometimes you are there to see another chapter of cricketing history made. So that ever afterwards you can tell people the story – in bar, office, train, taxi, kitchen or classroom. How you saw Bailey and Watson hold out for five hours, how Botham turned the game at Headingley, how Hollies trapped Bradman, how Griffin was no-balled for throwing at Lords, how C.B. Fry caught a swallow in the slips, how you heard the sound of Cowdrey's forearm snap. Dewy-eyed you can tell them 'I was there'. It is quite possible of course that they won't care. Members of your family and close friends may begin after a while to feel that they have been told about it often enough. Total strangers may enquire anxiously after your mental health and ask you who *is* Cowdrey anyway. It doesn't matter. The point is you were there, and you won't forget it –
however much everybody else wishes
you would.

One Day Cricket

One day cricket is as much about selling razor blades, the services of banks and insurance companies and cigarettes as it is about cricket. It cannot be denied however that the survival and indeed vastly increased popularity of cricket today all stemmed from the inception of the Gillette Cup (now called the Nat. West Trophy). This far-sighted piece of sponsorship rescued first class cricket from the doldrums. It was not long before other outfits jumped on the bandwagon and apart from the Benson and Hedges Cup we also have the John Player League, known universally as the Sunday Slog.

It is sometimes suggested that one day cricket is a new idea, which is nonsense. Until the five day Test matches and three day county matches began, cricket always was, and still is, essentially a one day game. At its best, at club level, it is not in the least unusual for five hundred runs to be scored in a day without anyone feeling that the game has lowered its standards.

We must suppress our other feelings and be grateful to the sponsors. They must, after all, look back with pride on some of the memorable finals at Lords that have been enjoyed by so many millions of people all over the world, not forgetting Prudential and their World Cup.

Whether all this sells more razor blades, life insurance policies, bank accounts or cigarettes, who knows. But it has done a power of good for selling more of the game.

Fielding Positions

The illustration overleaf is not (contrary to appearances) a version of the Night Sky feature from *The Times*. It shows all the possible positions where a captain can put his fielders. Or indeed where some of them will go in any case, if it suits them. Fielders do actually have something in common with planets, in that they are continually moving but never move very far from their fixed points. However the spinning red ball at the centre of the cricketing universe is not as big as the sun. And the fielders' main intention is not so much to revolve around it as to catch it.

Of course, other than the bowler and wicket keeper, there are only ever nine fielding positions occupied at any one time, so there are limitless different constellations available. There used to be a position called Long

Stop who was put there to make up for incompetent wicket keepers. Now though, Long Stop seems to be extinct and his role has been taken over by Deep Third Man or Deep Fine Leg. The incompetent wicket keeper is not however extinct and is still a common feature of many fielding sides.

Fielding positions have wonderful names and can provide a quick and very satisfying means of confusing the uninitiated. Try them on something like:

'He's only got two gulleys now, Blenkinsop has been moved from short square leg to silly mid-on. The slips have gone back two yards, there is no mid-wicket. He has packed the covers and has two men out deep and only one behind on the leg.'

The test is to see whether they reply 'That should cut down the singles' or whether they back off nervously with an incomprehensible patter of their own referring vaguely to an urgent appointment.

Fielding can have its lighter sides. There was once an incident when a major in the Blues, fielding at mid-off, found the ball whistling through his legs and heading off towards the boundary. Quick as a flash he turned to the man fielding at extra cover, and barked 'Fetch it, Corporal'.

On another occasion when a magnificent six had sent the ball soaring into a nearby wood, the first fielder to set off after it was Fergus, a Yorkshire terrier. Fergie's beautiful, leggy mistress followed in pursuit, and she in turn was shortly followed by the captain of Hampshire. The players waited and waited and waited. Finally Fergie's mistress reappeared, grinning broadly, with the captain of Hampshire, who was wearing most of her lipstick. And last of all Fergie, proudly carrying the ball.

A Word About Wicket Keeping

A good wicket keeper will frequently end his career with permanently damaged hands and knees. Just ask Godfrey Evans to show you his. They used to put pieces of raw steak inside their gloves to protect their hands. Modern gloves are better constructed, and have the advantage that they can be re-used more often than the steak.

The wicket keeper will usually be a more than useful batsman, since he will have had an opportunity to judge the pace and bounce of the wicket more than any other fielder. An examination of the records will show that time after time a wicket keeper has come to the rescue of a side whose early batting has once collapsed. On the whole, the noisier and more histrionic a keeper is, the worse he is. All except the Australian Rod Marsh who was noisy, histrionic, rude and brilliant.

Bowlers and Bowling

Bowlers come in three different speeds (fast, medium and slow), which is the only thing they have in common with old-fashioned gramophone records. They also come with either right-hand or left-hand drive, which is one of the few things they have in common with foreign cars. Most other bowling characteristics are unique to bowlers.

Fast bowlers

These are the gladiators of the game and the glamour boys. They have to be surprisingly fit and often hunt in pairs. Famous partnerships roll off the tongue like the names of provincial department stores – Statham and Trueman, Lillie and Thomson, Hall and Griffiths, Gregory and Macdonald and more recently Holding and Marshall spring to mind.

Often the thinking between these 'pairings' is that one of the two will succeed in scaring the daylights out of the batsman. Then with the change of end and the change of style of delivery, the batsman's concentration will momentarily relax and, wham, he is out – to the man he actually feared less. (Sometimes, particularly to people who know about cricket by half-listening to the radio commentaries, it comes as a surprise that these pairings actually *are* two people, and that for instance there never was a devastating lady bowler called Lillian Thomson.)

Fast bowlers don't have to be tall. Garner is but many aren't. The main thing is that they should be powerfully built and able to convey a sense of panic in the batsman as they power up towards the wicket. Fast bowlers should have big backsides. Quite fast bowlers can make do with quite big ones, very fast bowlers should have very big ones.

Medium Pace Bowlers

These can be known as seamers, swingers, stock bowlers or by many other names. They usually succeed by making the ball perform subtle tricks in the air and move unexpectedly off its seam. They do best when the wicket is slightly green and the air damp. If the batsman is also slightly green and wet that, of course, is also an advantage.

Medium bowlers are modest, taciturn, hard working and superbly fit, and they last for years.

There is one category of medium pace bowling called Military Medium, which is particularly dear to our hearts. The Military Medium is bowled by Majors at Staff College and beefy Brigadiers who were once fast but no longer have the pace. However they go on for ever – mainly because they are usually the captain.

Slow Bowlers

These are the most interesting to watch, and they employ a wide repertoire of spinning techniques, ranging from the 'orthodox left arm' (performed with the left arm, hence the word orthodox), to the less orthodox-sounding 'leg spin' (actually performed mainly with the right wrist).

Spin bowlers can employ such classics as the Bosie (after a Mr Bosanquet who invented it) or Googly which is the modern word for it (after who knows what). This is a nasty little specimen that comes at you as if it were an off break but it is delivered with a leg break action. If you can 'read' it you are a top class player – as you are if you can bowl it.

There is another well known type of delivery called a Chinaman. No one knows why or cares. It is unlikely that it was called after the man who invented it. The People's Republic is not on the whole noted for the quality of its spin bowlers. Perhaps it is called a Chinaman because of its inscrutability. It is in fact a left arm bowler's Googly.

Off spin is widely used nowadays, but leg spin less so because it is very risky. A leg spinner on a bad day can lose a match in a few overs by failing to find a length. On the other hand on a good day he can win a match equally quickly. Flight (i.e. the height of the delivery) is as important as spin, and just as deceptive.

Spinners are men of great hope and subtlety, more emotional than the fast and medium men, and often more clubbable. If they are any good, their fingers will be worn to ribbons. Many of them hail from the Indian sub-continent.

Batsmen

Left-handed, right-handed, short, tall, thin and thick, great batsmen come in all varieties. Mind you, everyone usually reckons they can bat a bit, and indeed more often than not everyone does have to bat. Each will have his own style, his own stance, his special strokes and his special weaknesses.

Opening bats are usually the solid players – good, consistent, frustratingly hard to get out. They appear to dig in to the wicket, tensed over their bats, ready to fend off any type of bowling with equal aplomb, and successful ones are often there for longer than one might wish.

Next in are the showmen – the ones who go in for more spectacular strokes and leap more athletically down the wicket. Either they make lots of runs fairly quickly or they lose their wickets to headstrong strokes.

At the very end (numbers ten or eleven or so) are the least effective batsmen. They are not usually expected to do anything much except try not to make life difficult for the one remaining good bat as he struggles to make the last few runs for his hundred.

Of course at high class levels all the batsmen have to be either solid or showy – and even some bowlers fancy their chances. Arthur Morris, Jackie MacGlew (known as Adhesive MacGlew because no one could get him out), Geoffrey Boycott or the late Ken Barrington are some of the greatest batsmen of the steady run-accumulating variety. Bradman, Compton, Cowdrey, Dexter, Miller, Sobers et al were the stroke-making kind.

There is much personal glory to be gained from a good innings, whether it is Botham's famous hundreds against the Australians, or a solid thirty runs on a turning wicket, or even one particularly sweetly struck boundary against the Wanstead Loss Adjusters XI. The greatest satisfaction is when you know that what you did changed the course of the game, even if you did only make 10.

The most important thing in batting is to play with a straight bat. This is not an issue you should take up with the suppliers of your sports equipment (unless of course your bat really is warped). It is a question of your cricketing style. Although actually plenty of people manage to make lots of runs with a crooked bat.

Most of the classic batting strokes are self explanatory.

Stroke: Any deliberately executed shot. Also something you can induce in fragile spectators if you deliberately execute a shot straight towards where they are sitting.

Cut: A short sharp stroke played behind the wicket on the off side. Well played it can give you the opportunity for a Cut and Run. Something you could well have been waiting for ever since things started getting nasty out there.

Glide: A smooth, graceful, carressing stroke played off the legs. The sort of thing you usually look forward to *after* the match, with luck.

Drive: An elegant attack on a half volley. If it doesn't work, you can always drive to the nearest pub and try an elegant attack on a double scotch instead.

Pull: A pull usually takes the ball from outside the off stump over to the leg side. Towards opening time the pull of The Kings Head usually takes the players from outside, on the pitch, over to the legless side.

31

Groundsmen

Every club has to have some sort of a groundsman. In villages and the smaller clubs he is often one of the players, or several of the players, not always with much expert knowledge. The preparation of a wicket and the constant maintenance of the square or playing area can dictate the quality and often the style of cricket to be played. There can be little doubt that some groundsmen do prepare wickets to suit their own sides or players. Especially in Nottingham. There is no law against it, and there are certainly occasions when wickets have been deliberately watered or surreptitiously rolled in the middle of the night to suit the weather forecast.

A groundsman should be a true son of the soil, knowledgeable about grass and weeds and preparations to grow or kill both. He must also be knowledgeable about the weather and drains and machinery, and above all he must have the confidence of his committee (or at least his own side). It is perfectly possible to change the course of a game by mucking about with the wicket.

The groundsman must also read closely Law 10 which deals with such matters as sweeping, mowing, watering, re-marking the crease, maintenance of foot holds and sowing of footholds and maintenance of the pitch. It is in fact up to the umpire to see that he has carried out his duties before and during a particular game, but between games the field is all his.

Gnome-like, the groundsman lives in his little hut beside or behind the pavilion, surrounded by buckets of whitewash, bags of sawdust, petrol cans and broken stumps. He knows that he can change the course of a game with greater ease than can many of the players. What about that odd patch outside the off-stump? It wasn't there yesterday. Funny how the outfield is never mowed properly when the good stroke playing sides come to play against us. And is that wicket really exactly twenty two yards long and are the stumps entirely opposite each other and how is it that a sight screen seemed to blow over in the lunch interval just before we went out to bat? The home side seems to have hot water in their taps and our chains won't pull. Yes, indeed the groundsman is all powerful.

Scorers

Even though computerised scoring is fast approaching, the man or girl with the pencil sitting on the wicker chair, or sweltering in a fly-blown old box under the tree will always be a fixture on the cricket scene.

In the first class game a competent scorer is *de rigeur*, and has to keep track of time, run rates, taking the new ball, recording numbers of overs bowled etc. He has to accept all instructions given him by the umpire, as well as having to check his score sheet against those of his fellow scorers. There must be times when cricket scorers heartily wish that their job could be a simple matter of counting goals.

Beware, however, of a scorer who arrives with a quiver of sharpened pencils, different colour inks, rubbers, stop watches and an eye shade. His job is quite complicated enough as it is without an array of elaborate equipment.

At the lower echelons scorers are hard to come by. More often than not the players themselves are roped in to keep the book going. Things often go wrong. It is best to score in soft pencil so you can rub out or even add things when no one is looking. If no rubber is available the toe of a gym shoe can be used or you can spill tea all over the book. It is often surprising how a batsman knows more about his own performance than the scorer. 'I tell you', he will say, peering over the record, 'I got two singles in that over. And you've gone and put that six down to the man with the bald head.'

The scorer can also come in for some tension in his relationship with the umpire. A strain can set in, for instance, on those many occasions when the hapless umpire finds himself standing with one leg in the air signalling a leg bye and shouting 'Scorer' in a loud voice, only to find that the scorer has actually just gone round the back for a pee and left a nine-year-old in charge.

And then, of course, there is the usual row about putting up the score on the board. 'I can't watch the game and do the Telegraph' is the scorer's usual complaint, or excuse. Although of course, he can frequently be seen reading it when the game has lost its momentum. To shouts of 'Tallywag' he will shift himself, grumbling, from his seat, hang 301 up when the score is 103 and complain that it was only last week that he asked the secretary to get some more nines as he always has to use upside down sixes and they keep falling off the board.

Nonetheless, he's not a bad sort. And he's always asked to the dinner.

Umpires

The traditional picture of an umpire, sweaters by the dozen wrapped round his neck and a pile of hats and caps on his head, is a thing of the past. Today's umpire, in the better classes of cricket, looks more like a male nurse or a vet with his short white coat and his immaculate white shoes. He carries a wide variety of technical equipment such as light meters, watches, pencils, note pads, sticking plaster, spare balls, boiled sweets and devices to count the number of balls in each over.

Once the umpire's word was law. Now, unfortunately, the umpire's word tends to attract a string of considerably less polite words in response, either from the players or from the spectators. And now there is an additional critic lurking around to attack the umpire in Test and county games. Known as the television action replay, it has an annoying habit of showing, from time to time, that, even if the umpire's word is law, it did not tally with what the cameras saw. People who disagreed with the umpire's decision used to keep quiet and not mention it. The television action replay has not been brought up to have such good manners.

Being a good umpire has always been a difficult job. Without instant acceptance of his decisions cricket would quickly become unplayable, but it is not easy to stand still in the blazing sun for five days and never let your mind wander. And you can bet your last sharp pencil that the moment you slip into a gentle day dream about windsurfing on Miami Beach, or suddenly find yourself wondering whether you have forgotten your sister's birthday, your thoughts will be interrupted by cries of 'Owzat' and you will be faced with a controversial LBW, and the television action replay will be warming up for its revenge. An umpire's life is not an easy one. Indeed, one way and another, it is surprising how seldom serious errors are made.

There is an umpire in India at the moment who goes by the name of Reporter. Presumeably he is a Parsee, as the Parsees took the names of their employers in the early days of the Raj. Hence once India had cricketers called Contractor, Engineer and Major. It will be interesting to see if, in the future, there might be some Indian engineering consultants called Umpire.

In lower class cricket, the umpires are often recruited from the batting side. This might sound certain to cast doubt on their essential neutrality, but in fact it usually works out quite well, cricket being the game it is. In any case it makes it more difficult for a batsman who has been called out to accuse the umpire of a bias towards the fielding side.

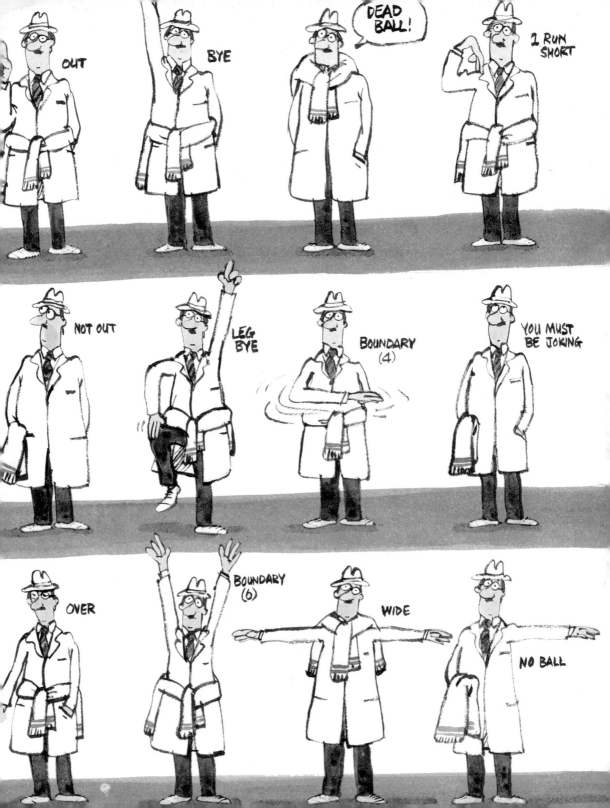

Cricket Teas and Lunches

In half day games, which include most village games, tea is generally the high spot of the afternoon. Indeed many clubs are known by their teas – and others by their tea ladies. Teas can range from hastily bought sliced bread with peanut butter to home-made cakes, hefty wholemeal sandwiches, sausage rolls and all the trimmings. It should always all be washed down with strong hot tea from a copper urn, preferably served through a hatch by several pretty girls.

More often than not it is the lot of the unfortunate captain's wife or the secretary's daughter to be lumbered with the chore of organising the tea. Other girlfriends and wives are usually roped in as reluctant 'spreaders'. The greatest nightmare is getting the quantities right. Buy too little and you find yourself cutting the bakewell tart into crumb-sized pieces to serve thousands. Buy too much and you have to live off fish paste for the next six months.

The best answer is often to develop a good relationship with a neighbouring pub. Building up this relationship is generally only a question of making them an offer they can't refuse i.e. 'If you help us with the teas, the lads will come back to your pub after the game'.

Lunches are a different matter. They range from the ridiculous (plastic ham and lettuce), to the sublimely unsuitable (sophisticated quiches, pies, patés and trifle with a liberal quantity of good wine and rounded off with vintage port). The latter are rarely conducive to a rewarding afternoon's session, but they can add greatly to the pleasure of the day as a whole. Particularly at charity matches where the cricket plays second fiddle to the razzamatazz and the high-scoring catering.

Lunch can in fact be used as an effective tactical weapon in cricket. The side you want to be particularly wary of playing in this respect is the Wine Trade, whose tradition is for each player to bring with him at least one 'sample'. The home side is expected to provide the port. Players whose best cricket has been performed on the strength of the more generally traditional cup of tea, are liable to find that large quantities of Chateau Lafite, 1945, does *not* have the same invigorating effect on the quality of their play.

Pavilions

Pavilions come in many varieties. They range from the Victorian elegance and squat power of the Lords Pavilion to the ghastly motorway urinal architecture of Headingley, the decaying elegance of Canterbury, or the windblown, peeling stucco of Sussex's folly at Hove. Most of us however are more at home in an old wooden shed or a newly constructed one-storey, all-purpose clubhouse. The main point about pavilions is not so much having somewhere to change, but having somewhere to sit when it rains. This is after all what cricket is about a lot of the time. In view of this, it is amazing how rigorously most cricket club bars stick to the licensing laws.

As most cricket clubs have got richer, there has been a revolution in changing rooms. The old wooden structures have finally given up the ghost, blown over, fallen down or been vandalised. They have been replaced by rather more secure structures with notices on the changing room doors saying 'Them and Us', and bars and tea rooms which take 'No Studs' and fruit machines, television sets, proper kitchens, proper loos and draft Heineken.

One of the troubles with first class pavilions nowadays is that one does meet the most appalling people shambling about behaving as if they owned the club, claiming acquaintance with the great and famous, and standing up in front of you just as the bowler starts his run. Once places of great exclusivity, they now resemble a cross between the Stock Exchange and a railway buffet.

Give us back the old shack with the thatched roof, the cracked wash basin, the seats with lids and full of moth-eaten old pads, jock straps, broken and splintered bats and other dubious bits of long cast-off clothing. Give us back too the urinal at the back with the sloping piece of rusty guttering, attached to a piece of decaying corrugated iron carrying off the effluence to a soakaway under the pavilion – where old beer cans, more discarded clothing and a broken slip catching machine (circa 1920) quietly mulch away.

Commentators

High up in his eerie sits the commentator. He is afforded the best view of the game but has, nevertheless, to sit in a rather precarious, often draughty position up a lot of stairs. Usually commentary positions are end-on, either at the highest point of the pavilion or just to one side. The height provides the panorama and it is easier to interpret the game from behind the bowler's arm or the batsman's back. You can see how the ball moves, which is so important to understanding the game.

Not that in fact the television commentators ever actually watch the play much themselves. Good Lord no. They rely on a bank of monitoring screens from however many cameras happen to be covering the match. They do sit in swivel chairs so that if they get a momentary let up (say at the fall of a wicket) they can turn round for a quick glimpse at the field of play – but only, of course, when not much of any interest is happening out there. Most of the time they sit with their headphones clamped on, their gazes firmly fixed on the monitors, moving from one angle to another at the producer's will.

Not only are the conditions under which the Benauds, Wests, Lewises and Dexters work cramped and inconvenient, they also require a special sort of person – one who knows when not to talk and who lets the action

speak for itself. Like night animals at the zoo they tend to look out of place when they emerge into the daylight to sum up the day's play, their backs to the field, blinking in the unaccustomed sun. They stand close together, filling the screen, uttering hastily cobbled together homilies which always begin, 'Well, Ted, I thought it all went India's way today . . .'. And they hope that the correctly edited clip will appear on their own monitor to enable Ted to say 'You're quite right Peter – as I said at lunchtime India are going to have a tough afternoon.'

The radio men live under even worse conditions. In small hutches on hastily erected scaffolding they crouch four to a box, assisted by long-suffering and professionally dumb scorers. They are surrounded by half-consumed cups of tea, curling sandwiches, half-eaten cakes (sent in by grateful listeners) and piles of unanswered and unanswerable letters. They have to talk us through hours and hours of inaction, occasionally relieved by a little burst of action, and somehow make it all seem equally gripping.

Test Match Special has become a sort of religion among radio listeners, many of whom would never consider going to an actual cricket match, but who share in the jokes with Jonners and Blowers and the Alderman as if they themselves were in the commentary box.

Cricket commentating provides ample time for reminiscence, waffle, completely irrelevant anecdotes and other essentials of the broadcaster's art. On the whole the men who do it make a splendid job of it, and indeed positively come into their own when it is raining or in the lunch and tea intervals when there isn't any actual cricket to interrupt the chat.

Since the war the art of radio commentating has developed until it is light years ahead of that on any other sport. The broadcasters themselves are almost a national institution . . . 'as I was only saying the other day. . . .'

Women and Cricket

Cricket was originally taught in girls' schools as much as anything else to instil the virtues of fair play and to ensure the girls had at least enough knowledge of the national game to sustain an ordinary conversation. The idea that any of the girls might actually get any good at it was not really considered. But in fact there is little to prevent a girl from getting good at cricket, provided she is prepared to risk having her teeth knocked out and her fingernails split in the pursuit of sport, and provided she can keep her 36B cup strapped out of the way of her bowling arm. Women's cricket has indeed now achieved enough status to assault the stuffy bastion of Lords, and it flourishes not only in the United Kingdom and the Commonwealth but also in Scandinavia and Holland. They have Test matches and international tours and of course, their own heroines. Most people have heard of Rachael Heyhoe-Flint. In fact many people think women's cricket was invented by Rachael Heyhoe-Flint. Some people think Rachael Heyhoe-Flint *is* women's cricket.

As well as actually playing cricket, women become heavily involved in it in many other ways. In a support role they do teas (see Cricket Teas and Lunches) and lunches (see Cricket Teas and Lunches) and laundry. (Note the man with the grey shirt and wearing cords in amongst all those washing powder advertisement whites. He's the one whose wife forgot to pick up his kit from the cleaners.)

Also, as a woman, you have to spectate, nobly. Up with the lark, you find yourself reminded once again that rough winds not only shake the darling buds of May but keep on shaking everything throughout June, July, August and September. Bravely undeterred you drive a hundred miles, to find the pitch ankle deep in water. So you spend all day sheltering in a corrugated hovel struggling to chat animatedly about run rates and left arm bowlers. When you stumble out through the rain to the lean-to loo you can overhear the men talking about you. 'Got stuck with that old boot for hours' you

hear, from that shy fellow you have spent such patient ages trying to bring out.

Spectating at Test matches has different hazards, although there is the possibility that it will be hot and that you will be able to strip down a bit and improve your tan. There are, of course, more comfortable sun bathing spots than the stands at the Oval, but there are worse things you can do in the stands at the Oval than sun-bathe. Such as trying to get to grips with the cricket. Test matches that run their full turn are rather like the Ring. Once, several days into a Test match, one poor girl was wandering dazedly around with her boyfriend looking as though she was sleepwalking. 'Don't worry,' he was saying, 'You'll get the hang of it by the end day.'

Punch-drunk with the Wagnerian tortuousness of it all, women all over the stands can often be heard saying things like 'Why are they clapping now? Oh, he's putting his sweater on.' Going to Test matches can not only put a serious strain on a girl's romantic relationships, it can, in time, actually threaten her sanity.

This said, there are plenty of genuinely keen women cricket supporters, who can cite Wisden at you on which touring side made a dramatic recovery in 1957, and who would go to Headingley of their own accord for no other reason than actually to watch the cricket. Some of the best cricket historians are women. And indeed, what great cricketer will not tell you how his mother would bowl at him for hours on the lawn at home and how his sister did all the fielding? Where would the men be without the lady scorers, the tea ladies or the adoring lady supporters on the boundary? Women are more essential to cricket than many of them (and than almost all men) know.

Cricket Tours

The less said about these the better. There are, of course, the grand tours made by the Test teams. These tours must be a constant nightmare for the participants. They spend three months living out of suitcases, moving by often inadequate transport from one end to another of a foreign land, suffering from strange tropical ailments and hideous sunburn. They are deprived of female company and are under the constant threat of political assassination, coups, monsoons and riots. And imagine what it must have been like touring Australia before the days of aircraft. And fancy being cooped up for six weeks on a boat with Douglas Jardine. Of course in those days there would have been strict segregation between the professionals and the amateurs, but that can't have helped much.

However, the tours that most of us are more familiar with, and that tend to stick in the mind are the rather less exalted variety. These expeditions set off to the farthest corners of the land, ostensibly to play cricket against complete strangers. In reality they are a good way of getting as far away from home as possible and then getting very, very drunk. Stories of these tours are legion, and best summed up perhaps by the experiences of the man who went on a cricket tour to Ireland. Playing in a match against the Irish Army at the time of the war in the Belgian Congo, he fell foul, after the match, of the bottle. Having passed out in Dublin he was alarmed, some 24 hours later, to wake up in Brazzaville – surrounded by his erstwhile opponents. He was, he discovered, on his way to join the United Nations Peace Keeping Forces. The Congolese wisely decided to ship him straight back to Dublin, where his colleagues meanwhile had declared him a missing person and sent back to England for another off-spinner.

The Laws of Cricket

There are 41 laws of cricket and they are all sacred. They can be found in the back of Wisden under such headings as Lost Ball, Dead Ball, No Ball, Hit the Ball Twice, Incommoding the Striker, Time Wasting, and Player's Conduct. Thus it will be seen that most of the things one can do with a ball, or indeed without, have been thought of by the cricketing law makers, and on the whole forbidden.

'Lost Ball' is a good law (number 20). It is designed to prevent the sort of farce arising where the batsmen could carry on running for hours or days – clocking up an unstoppable score – while the frantic fielders are securing the services of ferrets to retrieve balls from rabbit holes, or borrowing a gun to shoot down trapped balls in treetops (which has been known to happen). The sentiment behind the law is that, while a stroke full pitch over the boundary is worth six runs, it does not necessarily follow that a stroke which leaves the ball unrecoverable should be worth a potential 600 runs or more. Seems wise enough.

(Not long ago in Africa as a ball sped to the boundary a lion emerged from the bushes and started to play with it. The Umpire refused the cry of

lost ball because he could, in fact, see the ball. What he could not see was that all the players had hastily left the field.)

The law therefore says that if the fielders cry 'lost ball' the batsmen cannot add any more to their score by continuing to run thereafter – six only shall be added to the score. The only point the law does not take properly into account is that the average fielder, on realising that he will have to climb a tree or put his hand down a rabbit hole to retrieve the ball, usually finds that the first phrase to rise to his lips is something rather more emotional and not quite as couth as 'Lost Ball'.

Another intriguing law is number 35 which states that 'the striker shall be out Hit Wicket if while the ball is in play . . . his wicket is broken with any parts of his person, dress or equipment.' It once happened to Len Hutton in a Test match when his hat fell on the stumps. It was a humiliating way to be out – stumped by your own headgear. Most first class cricketers now wear strap-on helmets or bat bareheaded.

The cricket laws do of course get exhaustively discussed in bars and clubhouses. But that has after all been happening for over 200 years and has proved an almost wholly academic exercise. In all that time the laws have hardly changed at all.

Records and Heroes

One of the favourite pieces of patter among cricketing bar-proppers usually goes something like 'I was at Leeds in 1922 when old Lionel Tennyson made 63 with one hand against Gregory and MacDonald'. To which the reply is almost invariably 'Are you sure it was 1922?' or else 'not Leeds, old boy, Bradford.'

Cricket records and tales of the great and famous account for hours and hours of conversation after, before and even during the game itself. Indeed some cricket heroes of the dim, dark past are still national heroes today. Who has not heard for example, of W.G. Grace or Felix or Ranji?

And records themselves, so neatly and clearly set out in Wisden, The Cricketers Almanack, provide endless scope for barside and fireside chatter. Over 125 pages are devoted to *Records* and provide us with fascinating information such as individual scores of 300 or more, 300 runs in one day, four wickets with consecutive balls, or six sixes in an over (just achieved for the second time ever by the Indian Shastri).

This section of Wisden is a goldmine for the fanatic. He will tell you that Hanif Mohammad made 499 for Karachi against Bahawalpor in the 1958–59 season or recount the oft told tale of the Clifton schoolboy who made 628 not out in a house match, an innings of 6 hours 50 minutes spread over four afternoons. The boy was called Collins by the way. He may then go on to tell you how Michael Harbottle is the only man ever to have made a century in his only first class appearance, or that J.B. Hobbs scored 61,237 runs for an average of 50.65 throughout his career, how W.G. Grace made 2000 runs in a season 28 times, how D.V.P. Wright took 7 hat-tricks in his career, how Hedley Verity once took 17 wickets for 91 runs in a day or how Colin Cowdrey has taken 120 catches in 114 Test matches. And so it goes on. The heroes don't have to have been first class players. Most villages and clubs will have a hero or heroes of their own. Great feats of bowling or batting of years ago will still be recalled with care and attention even if not with accuracy.

It is almost impossible to explain to the uninitiated quite what this sort of conversation means to the participants. To the outsider it can even, apparently – amazingly – be desperately boring. But it is perhaps summed up by those moving lines by Francis Thompson, a Northerner himself, from his poem *At Lords* which begins: 'It is little I repair to the matches of the Southron folk' and ends, hauntingly, as he recalls two great players of his youth: 'Oh my Hornby and my Barlow long ago'.

Cricket Culture

Cricket has probably given rise to more literature and illustration than any other sport. The cast list of contributors to Alan Ross's anthology, *The Cricketers' Companion*, is positively star-studded: Dickens, L.P. Hartley, Neville Cardus, R.C. Robertson Glasgow, Edmund Blunden, William Blake, Lewis Carroll, Lord Byron, Francis Brett Young, Siegfried Sassoon, Francis Thompson, P.G. Wodehouse and many more, all have at some time found their muse on the cricket pitch. It says something for cricket's breadth that it must be, surely, one of very few common bonds between William Blake and P.G. Wodehouse.

Because cricket is a game which allows time for contemplation, not to mention ample scope for purple passages, it has always attracted writers, including many poets. It has also brought out the would-be poet in many who are not really writers, and has brought out the real writer in many who are supposed to be journalists. The daily papers feature columns and columns of cricket reporting, which plunges into quasi-poetry at moments of high emotion, and takes the art of sports journalism onto a new plane. The work of John Arlott, Alan Gibson, Tony Lewis, Robin Marlar and Frank Keating offers a constant source of entertainment, taking potentially dry information about cricket and transforming it into the stuff that literature is made of by their high standard of writing and wit.

Not only is there a never-ending stream of cricket books, anthologies and reminiscences, but there are also plenty of drawings and paintings based on cricket. Cricket does, after all, have more visual charm than most sports. A picturesque game of cricket on the village green has been the source for many a gracious, romantic picture. Not so the rugger scrum, for instance.

Then again, you don't have to have the pretty kind of cricket picture. You can also get the witty cricketing cartoon for the kitchen. Or one of those old brown monochromes of men in white (very pale brown) with heavy moustaches and enormous caps posing drunkenly for a team photo circa 1878, to put in the loo paying homage to the sporting past of one of your forebears. That is the thing about cricket where pictures and paintings are concerned – it is so versatile. Also of course, from the painting point of view, the players stay much stiller much longer than they do in most sports, which makes them a lot easier to draw.

Cricket can arouse every emotion from rage or laughter to reverent worship, which makes it hardly surprising that it has been the source for so many and such varied works of art.

Traditions and Etiquette

Once the word 'cricket' was synonymous with fair play, correctness and good manners. It was traditional, if you were caught at the wicket to 'walk', without waiting for an appeal. Nor did you ever query an umpire's decision, however wrong it was. And you did not try to distract the batsman's attention by talking in the slips or standing so that your shadow fell exactly on a good length. Now however these traditions seem to be losing ground and many dubious tactics, that are strictly 'not cricket' are condoned by umpires and players alike. People have started realising that the trouble with being gentlemanly is that it can give the other side a better chance of winning. Particularly if they are not being as gentlemanly as you are. That is why, alas, the tradition of gentlemanliness has gone

into a decline, at least in matches where winning is crucial. It does still exist in some areas of cricket, however, where people continue to abide by the old cricketing etiquette that sport is less about winning than about being polite to your opponents. It may be quaint, but that is the nature of most traditions, and it has certainly got more to do with sport than has swearing at the umpire.

There are many other traditions. It is traditional to applaud (as a spectator) if someone from the opposing team plays well. Even if you are really annoyed. It is not traditional (as a player) to betray a similar level of emotion if you are instantly dismissed. Even if you are extremely annoyed. It is traditional to fly the MCC flag above your own club flag over the pavilion. It is not traditional to wear the colours of any club except the one you are playing for. It is traditional to cry 'Owzat' if you think the batsman is out. It is not traditional to tip the bails off the non-striker's wicket as you come up to bowl, when he is out of his crease. It is traditional to wear white. It is not traditional to play cricket in an old pair of khaki cords and a shapeless off-white sweater knitted by your aunt.

Many clubs and counties, of course, have their own private traditions, but all the greatest ones are universal to the whole of cricket, and are enshrined in the laws. The laws have been around, hardly changed, since 1744, which makes them therefore, the most indisputably traditional of all cricketing practices.

What Not To Do As A Spectator

1. Do not walk behind the bowler's arm: If you are not an experienced cricket spectator and this expression is new to you, you might suppose that the bowler wouldn't let you walk behind him anyway. He wouldn't want you interfering with his Googlies. What the phrase in fact means is that you shouldn't bob up and down in front of the sight screens trying to signal to a friend to meet you in the car park just as the bowler is running up to bowl. The batsman will, after all, be wanting to keep his undistracted attention on the bowler's arm and the ball. Unless you have good reason to suppose that he would be even more interested in going to meet you in the car park.

2. Do not applaud extras or mis-fielding: This is the height of bad form, particularly if the match is delicately poised and the extra really is a piece of joyous news. The only time you can safely applaud an extra is when one side actually wins as a result of, say, a wide or a leg bye, in which case your applause may be taken as general approval for the result of a match (which you *are* allowed to be pleased about).

3. Do not run onto the ground: Neither age nor nationality can ever give you an excuse for crossing the boundary line at any time during a match. The fact that it is now an everyday occurrence does not make it acceptable.

On certain grounds it is permitted to stroll on the outfield and even run about with a tennis ball in the luncheon and tea intervals. But only by invitation and with official approval.

Although it is not permissible to walk on the pitch after the match, it is a good idea to go and stare at it. People will think you know more than they do. Especially if you can manage a few wise, non-commital grunts.

4. Do not flash: Beware the little looking glass taken from your handbag to check up on how brown you are getting. It might flash the sun into the batsman's eyes. Likewise be careful where you leave your car windscreen, for the same reason. Under this section it might also be worth mentioning that streaking is unwise at cricket matches. You might catch your balls on the bails.

5. Do not make too much noise in the stands: Never play your transistor too loud, particularly if it is tuned in to Lords and you are at the Oval. Try not to talk in the middle of a bowler's delivery. If you do, the commentators can't make their traditional comment of '. . . and there's a hush all around the ground as he comes in to bowl.' Don't bang beer tins together or beat drums unless, owing to your upbringing, you can't help it.

6. Do not attempt to initiate relationships with strangers: Be careful never to talk to your neighbours until you have ascertained where they are from, whether they are sober, and which side they support. If the information on all these points emerges as satisfactory you can then, cautiously, ask them a few sociable questions such as where they are from, who they support, and, if everything goes particularly satisfactorily, whether they would like to join you for a drink.

7. Do not go to the lavatory: Be sure never on any account to do this. If you ever do you can be absolutely certain that the one and only really exciting drama of the day will take place at that moment. And you will be sure to find that the windows are just too high to allow you to get so much as a glimpse of it.

Terms and Expressions

Cricket has its own language and if you want either to understand the game or to make sure that no one else understands you, it is important to learn the jargon. Here are some (but by no means all) of the best known cricketing terms.

Extras: These are runs such as byes and wides that are not made in the normal way, but are scored because someone on the fielding side has made a cock up. Extras is also the word used on an expenses sheet, after a cricketing tour, to describe areas of your expenditure you would prefer not to explain in detail.

Bye: This is an extra. If you manage to run a run without hitting the ball, that is a bye. Four byes are scored if the ball goes over the boundary without you hitting it. If this happens too often, the fielding captain will probably say bye bye to the wicket keeper.

Leg Bye: This is a run scored by your leg. If the ball hits your pad when you are attempting a stroke, and you are then able to make a run, that is a leg bye. If it hits your pad and you are then *not* able to make a run, that is more likely to be a different kind of cricketing situation called a leg injury.

No Ball: No-Balls are called when the bowler's foot is over the crease when he bowls. The bowler should not take it personally. It is not a comment on his private qualities.

Wide: A wide is called if the ball is bowled too wide. Also, more rarely, and considerably more surprisingly, if it is too high. Then it is called an overhead wide – just in case you thought there was anything too obvious about this piece of jargon.

Over: This is six deliveries from one end. When one over is over, everyone changes over and the next over begins.

Leg Spin: Not, in spite of appearances, a manoeuvre borrowed from ballroom dancing. This is a delivery that deviates deliberately from leg to off. (Some ballroom dancers also do this of course, but that is by the way.)

Off Spin: The opposite of a leg spin. Not to be confused with a spin off, which is what cricketers enjoy when they get paid for advertising aftershave or dog biscuits on television.

Full Toss: This is a delivery that arrives straight at the batsman without bouncing. Spectators watch to see whether it throws him into the air, and if so whether he comes up heads or tails.

Long Hop: This is when the bowler pitches the ball half way down the wicket or close to his own toes. If he pitches it too close to his own toes of course he is likely to find it a painfully long hop back to the pavilion.

Yorker: A cleverly pitched ball that lands in the block-hole, springs up underneath the bat and hits the wicket. Has been known to make the batsman spring up and down on his bat and hit the wicket keeper.

Grub: A prep school speciality. The ball is rolled along the pitch, which is not against the rules but is devilish to play. Like many prep school habits, however, it is not to be encouraged.

Googly or Chinaman: A delivery that bears much the same relation to normal bowling as Chinese script does to English. It goes in unexpected directions and is almost impossible to interpret.

Owzat: This is cried by the fielders to intimidate batsmen and umpires in an attempt to make sure the batsman will be out. It is called 'appealing', but it isn't very. It is really a rather bad mannered version of 'How's That?'